# Origins

# Get Me Out of Here!

Elen Caldecott ▪ Jonatronix

OXFORD
UNIVERSITY PRESS

**Uncle John**

## Venus flytrap

The Venus flytrap is a death trap for insects and spiders! The leaves have short, stiff hairs on them. When an insect or spider crawls on the leaves and touches the hairs the leaves snap shut. The plant then dissolves its prey for food.

# Chapter 1 – The garden jungle

*SNAP!*

"Wow! What is that?" Max asked.

His Uncle John grinned. "Scary, isn't it? It's a Venus flytrap. It's one of the few plants that eat animals. Usually it's the other way around!"

They were in Uncle John's greenhouse. A fly wriggled, trapped in the jaws of the Venus flytrap.

"Cool!" Tiger said.

"It's gross," Cat said, wrinkling her nose.

"I'm sure this plant is going to win a prize for me," Uncle John said proudly. "I'll win the best plant prize, for certain. No one else in my street will have anything like it. Most people show daffodils and sunflowers."

Uncle John turned to leave. "You can look around while I fetch some drinks."

As Uncle John walked past one of his plants, he gasped. "Oh, no!"

"What's the matter?" Max asked.

"Look at the leaves! They are ruined!"

The children looked at the plant. There were holes in some of the leaves. Others were turning yellow.

Uncle John looked upset. "This could ruin everything! If all the plants get sick, then there's no way I'll win the prize." He left the greenhouse looking very worried.

Max looked at Cat, Ant and Tiger. "We have to help my uncle. He loves his plants. We have to stop whatever it is that's hurting them."

"How can we help?" Tiger asked. "I don't know anything about gardening."

Ant looked thoughtful. "Lots of things might be causing the damage. It could be bugs or maybe a fungus. We'll have to take a closer look."

# Chapter 2 – The search for clues

The children turned the dials on their watches.
They pushed the X and ...

Plants and flowers towered over the children like trees in a rainforest. Vines hung down, thick as snakes. On the bench above them, the Venus flytrap's jaws glinted like crocodile's teeth.

"Come on," Max said. "Let's climb up there. We need to get on the bench." He pointed to a trellis which the children could climb like a ladder. One by one they climbed up carefully.

Max forced a path along the bench through the
green tangle, pushing the heavy leaves aside. They
trekked deeper and deeper into the undergrowth.

"Yuck!" Max said suddenly.

"What?" Cat asked. "Did you find a fungus?"

"I don't know what it is! It's something slippery
and slimy." Max reached out.

"Don't touch it!" Ant said urgently. "We don't know what it is. It might be dangerous."

"Do you think the slime is causing the problem?" Cat asked.

Ant kneeled down to look at it. "Maybe," he said thoughtfully.

# Chapter 3 – Tiger's fall

"Hey! Look at this," Tiger yelled.

Ant stood up. The others turned around.

Tiger had found one of the pieces of cork that Uncle John used for potting. He climbed up on top of it. "It's springy!" Tiger shouted, jumping up and down.

"Careful!" Max exclaimed.

Tiger leaped higher into the air, his arms stretched up above his head. "This is fun!"

*SNAP!*

The jaws of the Venus flytrap closed. Tiger yelled. He whipped his hand away. The plant's teeth locked together. It had just missed Tiger's fingers!

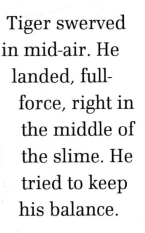

Tiger swerved in mid-air. He landed, full-force, right in the middle of the slime. He tried to keep his balance.

He threw his arms out, reaching for something to hold on to. He grabbed the cork, but it was no good.

Tiger's fall turned into a skid.
He swayed. He toppled. He slid.

"Tiger!" shouted Cat.

The children ran forwards to grab Tiger. But it was too late.

"No!" Max yelled, as Tiger tumbled over the edge of the bench. Down he fell towards the ground, far below.

Max, Cat and Ant looked over the edge. They were just in time to see the *SPLASH* as the cork, then Tiger, dropped into a bucket of water.

"Tiger!" Cat yelled.

Tiger bobbed gently up and down on top of the cork. He was still and silent.

"Tiger!" Max cried desperately.

"Ow!" The voice came from down below. "Ow! Wow! Wow!" Tiger said.

"Tiger!" Ant cried. "You're alive!"

Tiger stood up. The water came to just below his waist. He was a long way away, but they could just make out his grin. "That was amazing!" he shouted. "I landed on the cork. It saved my life."

"Are you hurt?" Cat shouted.

Tiger ran his hands along his body, checking for bumps and bruises. "I don't think so." Tiger smiled up at them.

Then Tiger's face fell. "I'm not hurt, but how am I going to get out?"

The walls of the bucket stretched high above him like prison walls. He waded to the side, to see if he could climb out. There were no hand-holds at all. He was trapped!

"What can we do?" Cat asked the others. "We have to rescue him."

Cat looked around. She saw Uncle John outside in the garden, putting the drinks down on a table. If they used their watches to grow now, he would see them. The micro-friends would have to rescue Tiger.

She looked along the workbench. Was there anything they could use? "Garden string!" she said. "We can use it like a rope. If you lower me down, then I can help Tiger climb out."

"Do you think you can do it?" Max asked.

Cat nodded. "I have to try."

# Chapter 5 – The rescue

Cat tied the rope around her body like a harness. Then she dropped over the edge while Max and Ant unwound the rope. The ground was a long way down. She took a deep breath. Tiger needed her to be brave.

She was lowered downwards. The rope creaked as it twisted from side to side.

"Go, Cat!" Tiger shouted excitedly.

Cat was nearly there. She was just inside the lip of the bucket. She could almost reach Tiger.

Then the rope stopped.

"What's the matter?" Tiger shouted.

"We've reached the end!" Max shouted back. "There's no more rope!"

"But I can't reach Tiger," Cat said, horrified.

She looked up. Max was staring down at her, looking worried. Ant was nowhere to be seen.

Then Ant was back. He was rolling something heavy across the workbench. It was the hosepipe nozzle!

Ant angled it over the edge. "If the rope won't reach Tiger," Ant said, "then Tiger will have to reach the rope! Everyone hold tight!"

Ant ran back to the tap and switched it on.
Seconds later, a stream of water fell past Cat and
into the bucket. Tiger grabbed the cork and dived
out of the way. The water crashed into the bucket.

The water level started to rise!

Tiger, clinging to the cork and using it like a float, rose with it.

He was getting closer and closer to Cat.

She reached down, stretching her fingers out as far as they would go.

Tiger's hand clasped tightly in hers.

"Got him!" Cat yelled.

Above them, Ant turned off the water.

Cat pulled as hard as she could. Tiger reached up and grabbed the rope. He was out of the water! Max and Ant pulled the rope up and, together, Cat and Tiger swung away from the bucket. Max and Ant lowered the rope a little and Cat and Tiger dropped safely on to a plant pot. From there they both climbed down to the ground.

# Chapter 6 – The plant munchers

Tiger stood on the floor next to the bucket. There were puddles of water around him. He was soaking wet.

He could see the workbench high above him, like a cliff top. He could see something else, too.

"Hey!" Tiger cried eagerly. "I think I've solved the mystery!"

A slime trail led along the ground. There, under the workbench, was a group of snails. They were huddled in a shady corner.

Max looked out at the garden. Uncle John was sitting down. He had his eyes closed and was snoring gently. "It's safe to use our watches. Uncle John is fast asleep."

The children turned their dials.

"Here are the culprits!" Tiger said. He reached down and picked up the snails that had been munching at the plants. "Uncle John should win the best plant prize now!"

Cat looked at Tiger. His clothes were dripping water on to the floor. "How are we going to explain this to Uncle John?" she asked.

Tiger grinned. He looked at the bucket full of water. He looked at his friends. "There's only one way," he said. "WATER FIGHT!" Tiger picked up the bucket and chased his friends out into the garden.